Finding My Way Home

poems by

Heidi Seaborn

Finishing Line Press
Georgetown, Kentucky

Finding My Way Home

ACKNOWLEDGMENTS

Grateful acknowledgement to the following publications where some of
these poems previously appeared:

3Elements Review: "Stung"
American Journal of Poetry: "Mani Pedi Sestina"
Caesura: The Poetic Games: "The Square House—94 Shaker Road, Harvard,
      Massachusetts"
Freshwater Magazine: "Ode to the Athlete" and "Shore Leave"
Fredericksburg Literary and Art Review: "How to Hold a Heart," "Separation"
      and "In Memoriam"
Gravel Magazine: "Submission Guidelines"
Into the Void Journal: "Small Deaths"
Nimrod International Journal of Poetry and Prose: "Family Secrets"
Oberon Poetry Magazine: "Keepsakes"
Timberline Review: "A Drift of Fishermen"
The Voices Project: "Break this Sentence Down: She Is Caught in a Loveless
      Marriage"
Vine Leaves Journal: "When We Fight"
West Trade Review: "Finding My Way Home" and "Hypothermia Survival
      Guide"
Windfall, A Journal of Poetry and Place: "But How Could We Forget?"
Seattle Poetry on Buses: excerpt from "But How Could We Forget?"
(Continued on Page 30)

Publisher: Leah Maines
Editor: Christen Kincaid
Cover Art: Rhonda Porter (photo), Nicky Sinclair (Concept)
Author Photo: Rosanne Olson
Cover Design: Elizabeth Maines McCleavy

Printed in the USA on acid-free paper.
Order online: www.finishinglinepress.com
         also available on amazon.com

Author inquiries and mail orders:
Finishing Line Press
P. O. Box 1626
Georgetown, Kentucky 40324
U. S. A.

Table of Contents

~For Jack, Hallie and Nicky
who are well on their journey
and for Scott, who is home to me.

Lost

The boat is adrift; it is
On fire
—Charles Wright

Hypothermia Survival Guide

The ice underfoot keens, then cracks,
a thunderclap, swallowing you.

You surface, your breath rises.
You have one minute to pace it.

> *I crawled from a snow shelter*
> *barefoot. My brain a sub-zero snarl,*

Ten minutes before muscle and nerve fibers freeze.
Flutter kick, float. Howl a wolf snared.

> *Dead of night. Dead of winter. Dead cold.*
> *Snow shifted into a river through my thighs.*

In one hour, you'll lose consciousness.
Before that you'll have forgotten your name.

> *A girl I barely knew, spooned me*
> *as a lover until my naked body hummed*

> *thermal,*
> *my eyes blinked open, lips pinked. Nerves lit.*
> *my vitals, my seared skin.*

Your crazy sets in, groans for somebody

to haul you from the suck of dreams,
stripped to a husk, cradled, as you burn back alive.

Family Secrets

1

The trees had stopped fruiting years ago,
the orchard reduced, home by home.

My tree was the third one in back, husked
to this patch of land that shouldered

the island's reach into the lake below.
I'd found it at age seven. A running start

to grab the lowest branch with both hands,
swing, then hoist myself up. An easy scramble
to the highest niche. I'd unwrap a sandwich,
pull out my notebook. From there, I could watch

the sailboats kite across the lake, spy
on the neighbors as they barbecued, disappear

into the leaves. Leave my sisters to wonder
if I'd run away with the ice cream man.

2

I can't tell you
how the lies have piled up
like driftwood after a winter storm,

how I clamber over each log, steady
myself with an outstretched arm
before slipping onto the beach,

how the clear water magnifies
bleached clamshells splayed and split,

how they look like half moons, reflected over
and over until the seabed's a horizon on Jupiter,

how I long to fill my pockets with shells,
as when we were children, to sell on
our drive's end for pennies,

how our pockets emptied sand, spilled
across the bathroom floor, wet with toe prints

3
We buried it deep this time. Deeper
than the babysitter's bra, our brother's
Matchbox cars, the ugly photo of me
in glasses and flood pants taken at Long Beach.

We boxed it up last night, the whole
messy story written in disappearing ink
on papyrus, folded into quarters, shoved
into an envelope, stamped with red sealing wax.

We dug all the way to China, with our bare hands.
Dirt under our nails, the tell tale.

The Poetry Workshop
For David Wagoner

The poet invites us to get lost in the woods, so we do.
Off trail, *salal* bunched damp around our boots,
lichen-crusted branches cracking underfoot,
following his metaphor into the cavernous Hoh rainforest.

Winter storms off the Pacific wrested old-growth hemlock
and spruce. Root structures big as a two-man crosscut saw
lay bare, splayed black hands stretched to hold off dank mist.
Each massive trunk an ancient history held.

When it is my turn to lead, I take us deeper still,
to what remains carved out of this rough land,
a clearing now lost to giant sword ferns, rhododendron trees.
There I offer up my poem like a mossy stone.

The writers set to work—my poem becomes a nurse cedar.
Fungi spores fleck its bark. Maple seedlings curl out of rot.
One day their roots will burrow the rainforest floor,
create a colonnade of stilted trees from the decay.

For now, I've lost my GPS—my fine sense of direction.
I listen for the far-off rush of the Hoh River
to guide me to its tribal mouth washing into the Pacific.

Stung

I stirred a hornets nest,
shears jabbing into the brush.

Disturbing the murmur of their day,
I stood still; wait out their frantic flight.

Like when I told my then husband
"I don't love you," maybe never had

over a birthday dinner. Sunset's glaze
reflected off the gold earrings

I'd bought in Cairo. I too must have glowed.
Could see it in his eyes before

I spoke those words that buzzed
around his head. Before I pulled

at the fragile papery nest of our marriage,
pruned the underbrush to plant anew.

Break this Sentence Down: She Is Caught in a Loveless Marriage

She
She: is *not*
without he.
Add an 's' like the
shushing of a child
She enfolds he,
additive, entwined.
Of course they are in this
Together.
Yet he can stand
alone.

Caught
Snared in a small trap,
perhaps a possum.
The steel teeth
clench her foot.
Blood, pain enough to
cry out but not be heard.
Or tangled,
the quiet act of netting a butterfly,
easing her into a jar.
Her wings flap wildly, then slow,
a final flutter.
Yes, that's it.

Loveless
Love reduced,
Diminished,
less than promised,
desired, required.
Less
love.

Marriage

Separation
For my sister

Patterns set like garden rows
planted six inches apart and rotated,
starting with spring radishes, arugula and kale.

Patterns unbroken like dishes stacked
on kitchen shelves, cups and glasses
near the sink, plates and bowls
left of the stove. The order set long ago
in the fatigue and exuberance
of that first day in the dreamed house,
surviving a renovation, kids
pilfering for their own beginning.

A percussive household rhythm
 of laundry on Sunday evenings,
folded after dinner in front of the TV,
of Friday nights with friends,
Saturday yard work then dinner in town,
twice a month house cleaning,
quarterly financial reviews,
annual trips to Europe.

What happens now?
Keep the familiar as it slows,
a car easing along the gravel drive,
tires roll the rutted grooves
come to halt in the garage. Lights off.

Or tomorrow stay up all night.
Watch the moon shift across the scarred sky.
Fill a bowl with hot milk and espresso
to greet the sunrise as if you lived in Paris.

In the afternoon I will come with my garden gloves
to help tear through the thicket
 left from a marriage rooted in routine.
We'll plant coneflower, forget me nots, gloriosa,
harvest the winter's honeycomb as the bees
hum a patient wait for the plum trees' first breath of spring.

In Memoriam
Chewuch River Valley, Okanogan County

Swallowed by a fire
that skipped borders,
shouldered roads, bridged
rivers, flicked, flamed, licked its way across
ranches, farms and fishing cabins,
leaving a black streak like tar
smeared by the hand of God.

Scorched ponderosa trees remain
blackened fingers in the cloudless sky.
Fields of flamboyant pink fireweed bloom
from gnarled, charred hunks and seared earth.
Wild roses, chaparral
grow beneath clutches of aspens.
Light sifts through ripe green leaves.

Keepsakes

He is aging in place.
The place being his home at the end of the road,
where time settles like silt on the knick-knacks
set long ago by his wife on the dresser, bed table.
Once a week, she'd lift each porcelain figure to dust,

recall its heritage. He remembers none of it.
Not the Dutch shoe from their trip to The Hague.
Not the Christmas when the angel arrived wrapped
by their children and tucked under the tree.
Not even the Cupid he found in a thrift store,
slipped into her coat pocket on Valentine's Day.

He knows only the weather the day Roosevelt
declared war. While his sister made snow angels,
he crept behind deep drifts, firing BBs
at the damn Krauts. They scampered like rabbits.
Later he trapped one, tortured it with a stick.
Its squeals startled a flock of sparrows into the smoky sky.

Shore Leave

Dr. William N. Stone, Boston Harbor, 1869

He could diagnose the particular illness
from across the docks by the way a sailor
walked off the ship and down the gangway.

Rickets: the scrawny bow-legged one.
Scabies: the short sailor, bag shouldered,
free-hand scratching vigorously.
TB: the mick's hunched, stalling cough.
Another hobbled by gangrene's deathly creep.

He'd ready the lotions, medicines,
scalpels, suture needles, bandages, whiskey.
Ready for bile-filled bellies, bones badly
broken then badly set. Mites and lice,
scurvy's blackening bruises, bloody
toothless mouths, wreaked livers,
weakened lungs, busted noses, cauliflower
ears, the ooze of puss from open wounds.

Steady stream. They'd queue outside. First stop
before pubs, whores, dinner, a bath,
while they still had cash in hand.

He'd ask them in to his room, seat
each sailor on the table. Quick check
then set to work, probe, mend, amputate,
medicate, bandage, eradicate.

Their breath stinking of rum and rot.
Their talk of storms, endless seas, loss.
Some arrived wearing death's ragged coat,
he'd refuse their pay. Peer, pry, then lie,
ply with more whisky and send off with a pat.

How to Hold a Heart

Instructions to my cardiac surgeon

Weighing in at ten ounces, the heart feels unexpectedly heavy.
You could palm it, but don't as it is slippery
with blood and the surprise that it pulses,
even later, as you lay it in a stainless steel basin.

So best to use two hands.
Hook your cupped palms together,
linking the pinkies, to create a basket
cradling the dislodged beating heart.

What will you do as it bleeds out?
Turn your back, ready the not-so-new new heart
as the nurse whisks away the old to the fire.
Or do you blink your eyes closed
long enough for inhale, exhale.

Long enough to consider me as your hand unfurls,
fingers graze my shoulder, assess my condition:
neither dead nor alive, heartless,
free from the expectation to love,
to be that perfect someone, that one and only.

But How Could We Forget?

The sea arrives steeping in a white porcelain bowl.
Mussels, clams, cod. A Dungeness crab claw
emerges from the tomato stew as if to say "I'm here."

But how could we forget? Summer evenings
the sun still high in the periwinkle sky as you rowed out.
I'd lean over expectant as Christmas,
haul the crab pot up hand over hand
seaweed circling my wrists.
Your gloved hand would dig into the skittering evergreen mass
knowing their weight and sex by touch.

This summer, we dropped your pot into the Sound on the highest tide.
Watched the buoy marked by your hand sink into the black.
I returned every day by kayak, stirring the sun off the water
to peer for your name lost amongst the kelp, your ashes.

We walk the pebbled shore; crackle clamshells as the fog hovers
obscuring Blake Island and the Olympics beyond.
The dog you will never know pockets crab claws in his jaw
buries them amongst the garden riot of zinnias, dahlias, and nasturtiums.

Found

You are surely lost. Stand still. The forest knows
Where you are. You must let it find you.
—David Wagoner

What We Hold On To
Dungeness Spit, Washington

The road gathers the fields, harvesting them with each turn.
A barn with silver silos crests the green horizon.
The houses, whose gardens snap sunflowers, rhubarb,
lettuce and stunted corn are the dream
we each harbor in the folded wing of our palm.

We stem from forest trail to the beach,
skid the sand between our toes,
feel the smooth circles of stone beneath our feet.
This spit is the crooked finger calling the ocean home,
the arm holding our family together.

We sleep on the driftwood,
eat cheese and sausage on Russian rye,
search for agates like four-leaf clovers.
The wind is not enough to unbalance the cranes from their post,
not enough to push us further down the spit to the lighthouse.

Submission Guidelines

Please do not send us a poem about birds.
We have no interest in the chattering

> of starlings flying over the burned field
> or the charm of finches that light

into your garden every morning.
We don't give two hoots about rooks

> in a clamour, nighthawk kettles, wren
> herds, magpies in a tiding or knobs

of widgeons and flights of pigeons.
We could care less that a congress

> of ravens is called an unkindness
> or for your poem about two unkind

ravens quarrelling on a telephone line
stretched in front of the sea. Speaking

> of sea, please don't send us poems
> about colonies of gulls or heron.

Especially no blue heron poems,
the world has too many already.

> Don't sneak a heron into your pond poem,
> already flush with mallards and paddling ducks.

God knows the world needs another
 nightingale poem, but call us old fashioned,

> we'll stick with Keats. We love
> the odd peacock sighting, but maybe

just a feather will do. Please refrain
from ostentation. Don't brood on pheasants

> or exalt the lark or pity the turtle dove
> or murder the crow. No sermonizing

on congregations of plovers or convocations
of eagles. No parliamentary oratory on owls.

If you do send us a bird poem, it better be good.

The Square House—94 Shaker Road, Harvard, Massachusetts
Built by Ireland Shadrach in 1769, the Square House
became the center for the Shaker community.

A square house rooted in a clearing of massive
broadleaf maples that burst into flames each fall.
A house built by a man who skipped the Revolution,
paid the King's taxes, worshipped god.

Neighbors said it was his ghost that lived with us,
the squirrel family in the attic,
hornets nesting in the nursery,
carpenter ants shedding wings, dying,
brittle carcasses scattered like a game of pick up sticks
and the mosquitos I'd kill at night creating a monotype
of smashed remains on the bedroom ceiling.

A house with a front door to nowhere,
a swing hung from a lilac bush the color of cough syrup
and a cat-tail rimmed pond buttered with lily pads
where I'd take my son to cup tadpoles and skitter bugs.

A house that held strong my daughter born
during the wail of a late May storm,
rocked her heavy, sleek body mid-night
to the click and whistle of crickets.

Small Deaths

The littlest creatures died quickly.
Goldfish lasted days, their glowing orange cadavers
bobbing on the fishbowl's murky surface.

The gecko survived a week. It's carcass
discovered one afternoon
dried up like a bug specimen.

The hamster stayed on earth long enough
to master the spinning wheel to nowhere,
to survive show and tell and the squeeze of chubby fists,
before strangulating on the cage bars in a botched escape.

The bunny arrived one Easter then died
days before the next, causing a resurrection watch.
When Hoppy failed to rise from the dead,
his corpse landed in the yard waste.

We never found the cat's body. Banished
to a life outdoors after bloodying the baby's face.
Perhaps it disappeared into the jaw of a ranging coyote.

We were not a family to bury our dead pets
with great ceremony in the back garden
under a handmade cross, whispering prayers

to serve warning to God's small creatures:
Beware. Enter at your own risk.

Ode to the Athlete
For my son with a nod to Pindar

Blessed is the boy. Grown tall long
before he'd grown up. Gifted boy,
an unexpected gift. The surprise
of an old soul born easily,
early to parents snared in life's
tragedy. He held fast at first.

Fingers tightly gripped my skirt.
His stories whispered in my ear
alone. Soon, the boy's dreams took flight.
His walk, a run. His jump, a leap.
Phrikias of the pre-school set.
Winged feet like Mercury,

he dashed to victory. To best
the boys race after race. His pace quick.
Each year, his share of prizes.
Then felled by injury one day,
wings singed, spirit smoldering,
the boy's mind collected his power.

He took gods' design, made it sweet,
a new beginning for a boy
now becoming a man. His hands
guide his imagination's strength,
reasoning. This race runs faster
at thought's speed. His competition

labors in the city's towers—
lit up at night like captive stars.
He knows the race of men, of gods,
that both breathe life from one mother.

Mani Pedi Sestina

The manicurist tugs on my ring,
rotates the diamond, wiggles it up snug
against the fat muscle and pulls. Nothing.
She soaps my fingers, leaving bubble trails,
to ease each band over my knuckle's hinge,
where they dry on the fresh, white

towel, in a neat stack. Leaving a white
tattoo, a pale reminder on my ring
finger of promises made, future hinged
at the hip-joint—ball and socket snug,
of golden champagne gulped, a trail
of bubbles kissing lips like nothing

more than air. Air kisses into nothing:
lips brushing past ears, the neat white
teeth smiles of women who now trail
into the salon, cluster into rings
like school girls, circular and snug.
Perfect heads, perfection hinged

to hair color, shoes, handbag, hinged
to a husband who will say nothing
about the hair color, handbag, shoes snug
against French pedicure-tipped white
toes adorned with a gold little-toe ring,
or her new clothing spilled in a trail

snaking the master suite. A trail
of pretty things, each hinged
to a life of glittering bejeweled rings,
where love is counted on fingers, no thing
withheld, wanting. Gleaming white
kitchens, bronzed bodies bikini-snug,

trips to private islands, mountain-top snugs,
where marriage is a transaction of trailing
annual dividends that skirt black and white,
color a world where doors burst their hinges,
against the swell of pretty little nothings,
of baubles, bells and glittering rings.

I slip my rings back over the fingers' hinge,
admire my nails as I pull my white sweater snug,
tip the manicurist. The women's talk trailing to nothing.

Body Politic

Flesh reflected.
Bleached winter pale.
Breasts weighted,
pocked by foraging
surgeons. Stomach,
a folded napkin.
Mottled crepe skin,
thinning, perpetually
shedding human chaff.

Slice. Peel
seven dermises deep
beneath follicle roots,
sweat glands.
Roll and pin back.
Strip away race,
ethnic identifiers. Naked
muscle, vein-threaded
sinew color of Georgia clay.
Strip away to connective tissue,
nerve, heart, lungs, guts.
Architecture. Brain.

Carve down
to the bone.
spine knuckled,
ribs, an emptied
cage. Pelvis
(where children
curled from seed
to spawn) splayed
open, gapped.
I stare
through vacant
eye cavities—
my skeleton
stares back.

November 2016

Thanksgiving, and the nasturtiums
are still in bloom. Persimmon

and pomegranate-hued flowers nestle
amongst leaves as large as my hand.

Seeded in the spring in a neat border
edging the grass, along the picket fence—

white, a little worn. My husband
slowly mends the fence, weather

permitting, post by post, slat by slat.
Now, the fence has all but disappeared

in the nasturtiums' tangled brush,
as vines winnowed months ago

under the fence and onto the sidewalk.
Passersby dodge our nasturtiums creep.

Some reach to pluck a bitter flower, take
a bite as they walk on down the road,

their talk of walls and borders, perhaps
just a fence or a bed of nasturtiums.

The Well-Endowed Dog's Lament

They are talking about my balls again,
my gonads, the family jewels.
"God, they're HUGE,"
she says as they walk behind me up the stairs.
 Yep. Massive," he responds, "even the vet said so."
"*Really*, did he mention it was time to neuter him?"

And there it is.
Just as I thrust out my shoulders,
lift my tail high, set those big balls
between my hind quarters
swinging from haunch to haunch,
she brings up the N word.

But he's got my back, at least my nuts.
"What's the rush?" he says, hand
slipping to guard his own crotch.
We watch out for each other. Sweetie and me.
That's what she calls him. Sweetie.

He calls her Honey. I do too,
when she gives me treats and scratches my chest
until my leg shakes, my whole body shivers,
even my contested balls
that must have a greater purpose
than for me to lick when bored.

It's a waiting game now.
Honey will win.
She will look at Sweetie
and his manhood will trump mine.
It's inevitable. The vet,
the cone of shame, the humiliation
of showing up at the park ball-less,
like every other dog.

When We Fight

I see the sinewy, sienna shoots emerge
from the flesh of his heels, sprout
out of his toes, worm their way through the carpet,
ferret weakness in the floorboards,
crawl under the door to join the insidious
morning glory spreading its violent tentacles
over our lush tended garden.

Meanwhile, I spit out words that flutter
furiously like Gypsy moths,
clutter the air around my face.
Their dusty wings powder my hair
before drawing to the light.
Burning bright, singeing wings.

Eventually, I gather up the broken moths,
scatter them like ashes out the window
onto the garden below. He dims the light,
pulls me under the bedding. Limbs
entwined like wisteria vines, our dreams
their fragrant bruised flower.

A Drift of Fishermen

It was always this way. Sea
edged in ice, lace doilies
crocheted to hold the stones.

Morning black and blue,
the lanterns' light blurs
with the fog lifting ahead of dawn.
A shrug of men, breath casting
ahead as their boats slip shore.

By the time I wake, the boats drift
grey flecks against the horizon.
The men will have emptied
their dreams as they bait, haul and gut.

Finding My Way Home

I was lost as the moon
on the night it disappeared
into umbra   charcoal   cold

waiting for the earth to turn
paint bloody swaths of illumination
excavate bones

a wait so long   I forgot my name
the way it fluttered
from my mother's mouth

a sparrow startled to wing
into a cracked-open sky
lost   years   decades

one night the moon slips shadow
harvests my name
from the constellations

pulls me over land
humped   shouldered
seas stirred black

time metered and shelved
to leave me with the morning tide
on this sun-bleached shore.

Acknowledgments Continued

"Family Secrets" was a semi-finalist for Pablo Neruda Poetry Prize 2017

"Hypothermia Survival Guide" was a finalist in the Cultural Center of Cape Co National Poetry Competition 2016.

"Submission Guidelines" was a Best of Net nominee for 2017.

"November 2016" is included in *Who Want the World as It Is Election Antholog* (Birds Piled Loosely Press, 2017).

"Body Politic" and "November 2016" were included in the political pamphlet chapbook *Body Politic* (Mount Analogue Press, 2017)

"What We Hold On To" is included in the Washington 129 Anthology (edited b Washington Poet Laureate Tod Marshall, Sage Hill Press, 2017)

Thank you to my tribe of poets who got me started on this journey: Lillo Wa Ken Wagner, Erika Brumett, Tige DeCoster and the Master Class of the Davi Wagoner at the Hugo House who gave me the advice and encouragement to writ and keep writing. Many thanks to my teachers and mentors: David Wagone Carolyne Wright, Jane Wong and especially to Veronica Golos for pushing m further than I thought I could go. Several of these poems were initially drafted a part of my participation in Tupelo Press 30/30 in November 2016. I am grateful t my fellow 30/30 poets and to my friends and family who supported that project.

My greatest appreciation goes to my husband, Scott Seaborn, for listening to eve the roughest drafts, and my mother, Denny Henkel who has been there from th beginning, lighting the flame.

Finally, thank you to Finishing Line Press editors Leah Maines and Christe Kincaid for their support and care in bringing my first collection of poems to life

Heidi Seaborn was brought up in Seattle, and returned in 2007 after thirty years of living, working and raising three children all over the world. She now can be found in a cottage overlooking Puget Sound with her husband and dog. Since she starting writing poetry in 2016, Heidi's work has appeared in numerous journals including *Nimrod International Journal* (2017 Pablo Neruda Prize for Poetry semi-finalist), *The New Guard* (2017 Knightville Prize semi-finalist), *Penn Review, Timberline, Gravel* (*Best of Net* nominee), in six anthologies, including *WA129* a collection edited of Washington's leading poets, as the political pamphlet/chapbook *Body Politic* published by Mount Analogue Press and on a Seattle bus. Heidi graduated from Stanford University with a degree in English Literature. She's a regular in David Wagoner's Master Class at the Hugo House, on the editorial staff of the *Adroit Journal*. Her published work can be found at: www.heidiseabornpoet.com. Twitter: @heidiseaborn1 Facebook: Heidi Seaborn

9 781635 344486